Watch Absolute Beginners!

How To Fix, Clean & Troubleshoot Timepieces For Fun & Profit

1st Edition

By George Piere

Table of Contents

Introduction 1

Chapter 1 - Introduction To Watch Making 2

Chapter 2 - Tools Of The Trade & How To Use Them 27

Chapter 3 - Practical Watch Repair (Common Issues & How To Address Them) 49

Chapter 4 - Cleaning & Reassembling A Watch 65

Chapter 5 – Proper Winding & Maintenance 78

Conclusion 84

Copyright

Copyright 2016 by George Piere. All rights reserved.

This document is geared towards providing exact and reliable information in regards to the topic and issue covered. The publication is sold with the idea that the publisher is not required to render accounting, officially permitted, or otherwise, qualified services. If advice is necessary, legal or professional, a practiced individual in the profession should be ordered.

- From a Declaration of Principles which was accepted and approved equally by a Committee of the American Bar Association and a Committee of Publishers and Associations.

In no way is it legal to reproduce, duplicate, or transmit any part of this document in either electronic means or in printed format. Recording of this publication is strictly prohibited and any storage of this document is not allowed unless with written permission from the publisher. All rights reserved.

The information provided herein is stated to be truthful and consistent, in that any liability, in terms of inattention or otherwise, by any usage or abuse of any policies, processes, or directions contained within is the solitary and utter responsibility of the recipient reader. Under no circumstances will any legal responsibility or blame be held against the publisher for any reparation, damages, or monetary loss due to the information herein, either directly or indirectly.

Respective authors own all copyrights not held by the publisher.

The information herein is offered for informational purposes solely, and is universal as so. The presentation of the information is without contract or any type of guarantee assurance.

The trademarks that are used are without any consent, and the publication of the trademark is without permission or backing by the trademark owner. All trademarks and brands within this book are for clarifying purposes only and are the owned by the owners themselves, not affiliated with this document.

Introduction

Becoming a pro in repairing watches entails a lot of practice and training. So, this book aims to make it easier for you to understand what you need to know about the construction of watches, the common problems they encounter, and how to fix them.

You can use this as a reference to understand the features and basic parts of different kinds of watches. It has dedicated chapters about the more technical aspects of watchmaking that you can try after you have familiarized yourself with the simpler concepts.

You can use the steps provided in this book to begin maintaining and troubleshooting your own watches. You may even apply what you have learned to make extra money.

Thanks for purchasing this book, I hope you enjoy it!

Chapter 1 - Introduction To Watch Making

Horology refers to the craft of making and repairing clocks and watches, and those who are involved in the process are called horologists. There was a time when watchmakers were also involved in the process of crafting the parts and creating watches. It has changed since the advent of factory-made watches.

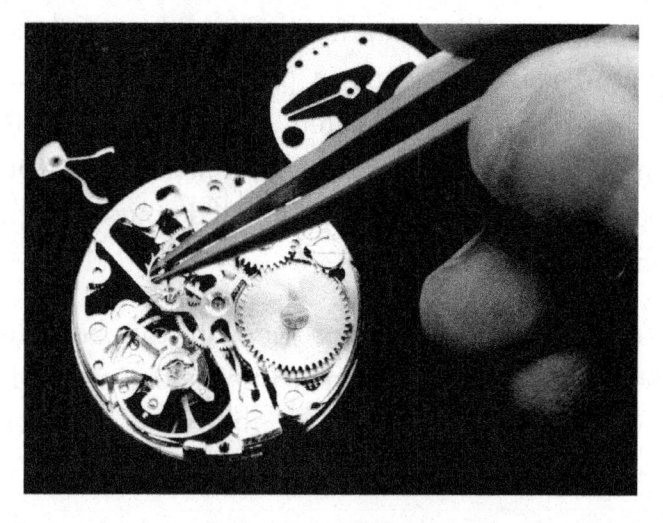

Since today's fashion watches are cheaper to replace than to repair, horologists now mainly cater to those who own expensive timepieces.

Many practicing horologists these days use their skills on recent production watches. Only a few offer services in fabricating replacement parts – it's much more common to get spares from the factory and fit them into the brand of watch they are working on.

Most watchmakers of this generation, specifically in Europe and Switzerland, are directly employed by the watchmaking industry. They are required to finish a related degree from a technical school. After graduating, they undergo in-house training from the company where they are employed.

The training and qualifications that you will need as a watchmaker depend on where you intend to work. For example, Rolex, which is a Swiss brand that produces high-end watches, requires their horologists to finish modern training and get the necessary certificates from a number of known schools. They also require their watchmakers to become a member of the American Watchmakers-Clockmakers Institute.

Due to the proliferation of fakes, majority of modern Swiss brands implement tight quality control. They do not sell watch parts even to the most credible independent horologists.

Horology is both art and science. Begin by perfecting your manual skills – learn how to delicately touch the parts of the watch or clock by maneuvering the muscles of your fingers and wrist.

How to Become a Horologist

1. Look for a pro and apply as an apprentice. The fastest way to learn the skills is to see how it is done by a professional and get a chance to try your hands in the process. It will not be easy to find someone who will readily agree, especially if you are aiming for a horologist who's known in the field. Still, your effort will be worth it in the end. The training will become an asset when you later on apply for a job with a known watch company. A pro can give you the right tips and reveal the tricks of the trade. The process might take longer to learn without the help of someone who's willing to share his/her genius.

2. Enroll in a technical school and take a formal watchmaking course. Most of the curricula take as little as a year to complete. They mainly focus on the mechanical aspect of watch repair, but you can get supplemental courses to widen your knowledge. You will be given a certificate after you have completed a course. This will serve as proof that you have passed standardized testing in the aspect of watchmaking that you have enrolled in.

3. There are certain schools and institutions that offer training positions in a two-year program certified by the Swiss American Watchmakers Training Alliance. Look for a location near you and inquire how you can go about the process.

4. There are two schools in the US, the N.G. Hayek Watchmaking School and North American Institute of Swiss Watchmaking, which offer a 3,000-hour course through the Watchmakers of Switzerland Training and Education Program. The course can be completed in a matter of two to three years.

5. Whether you intend to make this a hobby or you want to turn this into a small time home-based business, you can start teaching yourself about the technical aspects of the process. Reading reference materials, like this book, is a good way to begin. You could also take online courses about watch and clock repair. Take note that you still have to get formal training and

certification if ever you decide to work for someone else later on.

Looking Back

Before going about the technical aspect of watchmaking, here's a brief look at where it all began. It is a common belief that the measurement of time was first done by observing the heavenly bodies. The days and the months were first distinguished by observing the course of the sun and the moon. This has been the basis of age and the division of time. However, it remains a mystery how the concept of weeks came to be.

The first instruments used to divide one day into smaller portions of time were the sundials. The shadow that was produced when the sun's rays hit the sundial gave the ancient people an idea about the time of the day. These instruments originated from China, where astronomy was commonly practiced.

Even now, there are still certain places, specifically the ones that seldom use watches and clocks, where the time of the day is determined by looking at the sun. After the sundials, the next tool that was used to measure time was the clepsydra or water clock. It is composed of vessels that are arranged to make the water flow gradually from one vessel to another. The flow of the water indicates the flight of time. One form of the clepsydra is the hourglass, which utilizes sand instead of water.

Watches were first introduced in the 16th century. In 1542, the term "watch" was first used to refer to a timekeeper. The first item that showcased the distinction of a watch from a clock (with the former being a portable timekeeper) was the compass. It was used by the Chinese, and they referred to it as the pocket sundial. The earliest portable timekeeper that makes use of a spring was the Nuremberg Egg. It was invented in 1477.

The invention of pocket clocks in 1500 was credited to Peter Hale. They were described by historians as striking and something new, and were called Nuremberg Eggs. The earliest watches only had one hand and needed winding twice daily, although their arrangement was similar to those used in modern American spring clocks.

The first materials used in manufacturing watches were iron and steel. Watches that were made of brass came about in 1560. The original shape of the watches was oval, and the round-shaped watches were later introduced in 1610. Metals were first used as protection for the dial and hands, as glass in 1620.

Characteristics for Comparison

It's fairly common for timepiece enthusiasts to compare their collections, and they typically discuss the following:

- <u>Escapements</u> – lever, cylinder, duplex or verge
- <u>Case material (silver or gold)</u> – this can be easily checked if the Hallmark is visible. However, note that most watches manufactured in England are not Hallmarked. An experienced eye will still know the difference. If that fails, testing with nitric acid is also an option (although it could lead to damage).
- <u>The style of the case</u> – pair-cased, hunter, half-hunter, open face, glass or crystal
- <u>Origin (foreign or English)</u> – the popularity of English watches resulted in what many consider as creative imitation. You ought to inspect the cases to determine the differences. The bolt is pressed using a thumbnail in English cases, since the movement of the watch is attached to the center. The movement can be lifted after opening the bezel. The cases of foreign watches, on the other hand, typically open at the back.

Two Common Questions

Through time, you will get better at assessing the features and styles of watches by simply looking at them. For now though, it's best to familiarize yourself with the answers to these common questions:

1. <u>Is it quartz or mechanical?</u>

Quartz watches are activated using a specifically-designed battery. The battery activates the crystal found in the movement, creating vibrations of up to 33 times/second. These vibrations go through a chip, which translates them into impulses that drive the electronic motor of the timepiece. This causes the hands of the watch to move.

Mechanical watches, on the other hand, can be self-winding or manual. You have to wind the watch on your own if it is manual. If it is automatic, a rotor activates the movement that runs through the gravitational force that the watch is subjected to when it is worn.

2. <u>Should you go for trendy or costly timepieces?</u>

An expensive and well-made watch is considered an investment. It will last through generations for as long as you subject it to proper handling and care. Often, a timepiece's price is indicative of its longevity. Also, keep in mind that trendy pieces are considered disposable because they are, more often than not, cheaper to replace than to be repaired.

The price of a watch, regardless of type, is affected by several factors that include the materials used for the casing, the strap used, additional jewels or ornament, and the kind of movements it has.

Helping Others Make the Right Choice

As someone who's probably thinking of repairing other people's watches (whether free of charge or for a small fee), you should know how to advise your future clients properly when it comes to choosing the right timepiece. So, to help you out with that, here are some of the most important things you have to do whenever people ask you for pointers:

1. Remind them that there are different kinds of watches currently available. It's important for them to know more about the cost of a timepiece, and how it is affected by certain features and characteristics (such as the band and overall construction).

2. Tell them that it's important to check whether all functions are actually working. While it might be enough for some to see a list of functions, it's always best to double-check such claims. Don't forget to remind the curious that even in the watch industry, shady claims aren't that uncommon.

3. Inform them that when it comes to checking a timepiece's durability, it's necessary to gain insights from manufacturer ratings. Some brands are known for durability, but they're usually the ones synonymous with pricey offerings. Still, don't forget to tell your clients that watches with hefty price tags aren't guaranteed to be better than their lesser-priced counterparts.

4. Remind them that if a watch doesn't have any marking that indicates it is water resistant, it is safe to assume that it's not. Given that water-resistance improves durability and broadens a timepiece's potential uses, watch companies surely won't forget to highlight the inclusion of such an impressive feature.

5. Don't hesitate to tell them that the battery life of digital watches lasts up to 10 years (even if that means you will be getting fewer requests for battery replacement). Also, don't forget to advise your customers that checking the manufacturer's claims on battery life should yield more accurate estimates.

6. Here's one practical suggestion you should give – while it is good to invest in expensive models of watches, it's smart to have cheaper kinds for everyday use. Likewise, it is recommended to go for inexpensive timepieces with standard-sized straps. They are easier to replace than the wider straps that tend to be expensive and hard to find.

7. Tell them to be careful in buying watches because fake ones have become quite common. It's vital to inspect all the details and purchase only from a reputable source. Aside from that, it's best to avoid buying an analog watch without the markings. Simply put, if a certain timepiece seems too cheap given its brand and model, it would be wise to simply stay away from it as it's probably fake.

Most Common Terms in Horology

It is part of your job as an aspiring horologist to determine the kind, make, and features of a watch just by looking at it. To have a chance at successfully doing that, you will have to familiarize yourself with terms that you will encounter as you start learning about the process of watchmaking:

1. 12-Hour/24-Hour and 30-Minute Register

Also called the recorder, this feature is able to record time periods of 12 or 24 hours, and there are also certain watch models that can chart periods of 30 minutes. This is a sub-dial found on the front face of the watch.

2. Adjusted

This term is often used by salespeople. It means that the watch has undergone several tests during assembly. It has already been calibrated with at least nine adjustments to ensure that it will work properly after the owner has taken it home, no matter what the weather and other conditions are.

3. Alarm

This feature is found in both mechanical and quartz watches. It allows the user to set a time for the watch to signal an alert. An extra hand is sometimes added to allow for time to pre-set. A second mainspring is placed inside the movement, which sets a little element that causes weight to vibrate in a back and forth manner. This will create the noise or vibration that will last for a number of seconds, or until the alarm is turned off.

4. Altimeter

This looks similar to the one installed in an airplane's cockpit, and is commonly found in watches used by pilots. The feature is able to measure height above sea level by taking note of the changes in barometric pressure. Aside from being useful to pilots, this feature could also be handy for sky divers and mountain climbers.

5. AM and PM Indicator

This feature that's typically found on digital and 12-hour analog watches lets users check if it is already day or night.

6. Analog/Digital Display

This is also called dual display or anidigi. This is a common trend among fashion watches, but serves as an important tool for people in the emergency and military service. This function can help in performing duties, such as timing, synchronization and CPR, with much efficiency and ease.

7. Analog Watch

This is the kind of watch with hour and minute hands moving in a clockwise manner around the dial.

8. Anti-Magnetic

This kind of feature is now employed in many automatic and mechanical watches.

Magnetization, which can be caused by exposure to stereo systems, televisions, refrigerators, or cars, leads to the disruption of time. Alloy parts are installed in the components of the watch, such as the balance wheel or escape wheel, to counteract the magnetic field.

9. Aperture

This is a small window cut in the dial to display the date or day.

10. Atmosphere

It measures air pressure at sea level to indicate the water resistance capacity of a watch.

11. Atomic Calendar

This is takes into account the different lengths of months, including leap years. There are also certain programs that can be pre-set up to 40 years in advance.

12. Atomic Clock

This is known as the most accurate timekeeping device that utilizes the vibrations of atoms in a metal isotope. The user is only required to set the time zone, and the watch works through radio transmission.

13. Auto Switch Backlight

With this feature, the watch will automatically illuminate when you put it near your face.

14. Automatic Watch

This has a lot of similarities to a mechanical timepiece, except that the wearer's movements keep the watch running. This is made possible by a small rotor that moves along with the wrist. This kind of watch was first worn by John Harwood and was invented in the 18th century by Breguet. If the watch is not worn for 36 hours, manually winding it becomes necessary.

15. Band Width

It measures the distance of the lugs in the case. This comes in handy when you need to buy a replacement strap or band because it determines the size required for your timepiece.

16. Battery Reserve Indicator

This is a feature in quartz watches that indicates whether the battery will soon run out. You will notice the second hand of the watch jumping in four-second intervals. This is an indication that the battery will only last for about two more weeks.

17. Batteryless Quartz Watch

This kind of timepiece runs on a tiny electronic generator. The watch is able to keep time as it stores energy in the rechargeable battery that it is equipped with. It has to be worn regularly to avoid malfunction.

18. Calendar

The display option for this feature depends on the model of the watch. There are some that only show the day, while others show the month, day, and year.

19. Cambered Crystal

This feature means that the glass of the watch was designed in a dome-like manner.

20. Chronograph

This pertains to watches with a stopwatch feature.

21. Complication

The term is used to refer to additional features. Simple complications include calendars, alarms, and chronographs. Minute repeaters, tour billions, and perpetual calendars are more intricate examples.

22. Cosmograph

This has lots of similarities to the chronograph, but it uses a tachymeter that gives it a modern finish.

23. Depth Alarm

This is included in diving watches, and gives off an alarm through sound or vibration when the preset depth level is reached by the diver. It will automatically stop the alarm when the diver moves back to a safe position.

24. <u>Depth Sensor/Depth Meter</u>

The feature above works due to the measurement that this sensor provides. With the use of water pressure, the sensor allows the diver to monitor his/her depth level.

25. <u>Digital Watch</u>

This kind of watch was first developed in the 70s. It typically operates with the use of side buttons. It has become quite popular among the youth.

26. <u>Dimaskeening</u>

This refers to the process of carving or etching markings on the watch movement as an added decoration.

27. <u>Diver's Watch</u>

It typically has a minimum water resistance capacity of 200 meters, and comes with complications useful for diving (such as case back, screw-down crown, and rotating bezel).

28. <u>Dual Time</u>

Watches with this feature shows the local time and one other time zone, which is handy for business people and those who love to travel.

29. Electronic Watch

This is more commonly known as a quartz watch. It runs through an electric current maintained by a battery. Its quartz oscillator is capable of vibrating at 32,768Hz per second. The vibrations are processed until they are converted into an impulse that's strong enough to move the gear train. Some electronic watches utilize solar cells instead of batteries.

30. GMT Time Zone

GMT means Greenwich Mean Time. This is also called Zulu Time or Universal Time Coordinated (UTC). When it comes to watches, it pertains to the capability to feature dual time zones.

31. Hallmark

This is an engraving or stamp that contains information about the quality or the origin of the metals used.

32. Isochronism

This pertains to a mechanical watch that runs smoothly, even if it is not fully wound.

33. Liquid Crystal Display (LCD)

The term is also used to refer to digital watches with numeric Arabic display.

34. Luminous

A glow-in-the-dark coating is applied to the hands and other markers of the watch, making them glow when the watch is placed somewhere dark.

35. Mechanical Movement

It pertains to watches that are activated without the need for any electrical source.

36. Military Time

This is also called the 24-hour clock.

37. Mineral Crystal

This is a kind of synthetic glass with greater scratch resistance than plastic.

38. Oil Sink

It is a depressed pool around the pivot and can hold a small amount of oil that acts as lubricant to the gears.

39. Positions

This refers to the different tests that the watch undergoes to make sure that it remains accurate no matter what the position is.

40. Platinum

Also referred to as platine, this is known as one of the most durable metals. It is commonly used in making limited edition watches because the metal doesn't tarnish and looks consistently great for a long time.

41. Quartz Movement

This is another term used to refer to electronic watches. These timepieces are capable of charging or running with the use of batteries. They are not that expensive, but are known for their accuracy.

42. Regulator

It serves as a separator between the hour and minute hands in various sub dials and axial.

43. Screw Down Crown

This is an important feature in water-resistant watches. It has a gasket that seals the opening when the watch is exposed to water.

44. Shock Resistant

This means that the watch is capable of withstanding impact equivalent to being dropped three feet from the ground.

45. Skeleton Watch

This kind of watch casing has a transparent front and no dial. You can view the movement without the need to take the timepiece off.

46. Stainless Steel

This metal is resistant to corrosion. This is the second best choice for those who can't afford expensive metals, such as platinum or gold.

47. Swiss Made

This mark means that most of the parts and pieces of the watch, including the assembly and inspection, were done by a manufacturer in Switzerland. There is a law that requires that at least half of the components of a watch should be made, put together, and inspected in Switzerland in order to prevent the proliferation of replica Swiss watches.

48. Swiss Movement

If the watch comes with this marking, it means that only the movement is Swiss-made.

49. Tachymeter Scale

This is one feature of chronographs that can measure distance based on speed.

50. Titanium

This is now often used in diving watches due to its resistance to saltwater corrosion.

A Reference on Watch Brands

Before we move on to the next chapter (in which you will learn about the tools of the trade), it's only appropriate that you familiarize yourself with the different watch brands in the world. Remember, a timepiece's brand partly determines its value, and gives clues on how it was made. It could also provide insights on potential issues.

1. Audemars Piguet

Known for their ultra-luxury Swiss watches, the brand was established in 1875. Despite being among the oldest watch makers in the world, it is still owned by the Audemars and the Piguets (unlike many other century-old firms that have eventually been acquired by other companies for the sake of survival).

2. Breitling

Yet another brand with a history that spans over a hundred years, Breitling remains headquartered in Grenchen, Switzerland. While it has a wide assortment of timepieces for all kinds of enthusiasts, the watchmaker specializes in creating chronometers perfect for diving and for aviation.

3. Franck Muller

Tagged as the "Master of Complications", this brand has become popular due to the complex mechanisms and features of its timepieces. It even has yearly events in which new lines of watches are revealed, and every new lineup comes equipped with a never-before-seen complication.

4. Girard Perregaux

Among the most well-known watchmakers in the world, Girard Perregaux was established in the late 1700s. It has acquired numerous patents throughout the decades. It's credited for having carried out the first major commercial production of a timepiece, and for creating the constant force escapement.

5. Hamilton

While it did not manage to stay as its own company (having been acquired in the 1990s by what would eventually become known as Swatch), Hamilton is still a key part of watch history. It's interesting to note though, that its initial offerings mainly came in the form of pocket watches in gold cases.

6. Movado

Movado is among the most popular American watchmakers. Unlike many other brands that have become synonymous with complex mechanisms, this has become the very definition of simplicity and elegance. Most of Movado's timepieces only feature a single dot that represents the sun's position at noon.

7. Nomos

Headquartered in Glashutte, Germany, Nomos is a relatively young company as it was only founded in 1990. Nonetheless, it has been making waves with its assortment of manual and automatic timepieces. Its creations are made even more special with the use of in-house movements.

8. Omega

Despite being another brand that is currently under the Swatch Group, Omega has a rich history that spans over a century. In fact, the first watch to be ever brought to the moon was an Omega timepiece. The brand's offerings have also been featured in several Bond films.

9. Patek Philippe

Founded in 1851, Patek Philippe is a Swiss watchmaker that remains privately owned. The brand's offerings has been associated with luxury – its 5002P, for example, was sold for more than a million dollars. With that, it shouldn't be surprising that it's deemed by many as the most prestigious among watchmakers.

10. Rolex

Another luxury brand, Rolex was established by Hans Wilsdorf and Alfred Davis. The watchmaker wasn't initially headquartered in Switzerland, as its roots can be traced back to

London. Being among the oldest brands and catering to high-paying clients, Rolex remains among the most influential in the watch industry.

11. Ulysse Nardin

Founded in Switzerland in the 1840s, Ulysse Nardin is synonymous with top-of-the-line marine chronometers. At one point, the company was even the sole provider of watches to the naval fleets of various countries. Despite its success, the watchmaker has undergone several acquisitions throughout the years.

12. Tissot

A luxury brand, Tissot has been around since 1853. Interestingly enough, despite being associated with luxury timepieces, its parent company (Swatch) considers the brand as targeted towards the mid-range market. Do note that Tissot is not the same (and is not associated in any way) with Swiss brand Mathey-Tissot.

13. TAG Heuer

While most other brands on this list solely focus on manufacturing watches, TAG Heuer maintains a more varied approach in business. Aside from offering Swiss timepieces, the company offers fashion accessories and even mobile phones. Despite that, its timepieces (such as the Carrera and Monaco) remain top sellers.

Chapter 2 - Tools Of The Trade & How To Use Them

It will be easier to learn about the process of watch repair when you already have the tools ready. For starters, you can buy a kit that is complete with the simplest pieces needed to get things done. You can add more tools as you go along and as you learn more about the tricks of the trade.

Four Most Important Tools

In the beginning, make sure that you have these four. Don't think about sacrificing quality as you'll be using them often.

1. Gravers

They are used for turning the lathe. Gravers are typically made of hardened Swedish steel, and are sharpened using an Arkansas stone with a bit of Pike oilstone. Hold a piece like how you would a pencil. Move it in a sweeping motion and then use it to grind according to the shape that is found in the manual. There are gravers, especially the recently-made ones, which contain carbide. Carbide is an extra hard alloy that is brittle and chips easily. You cannot use gravers with carbide in grinding a long point.

2. Eye loupe or eyeglass

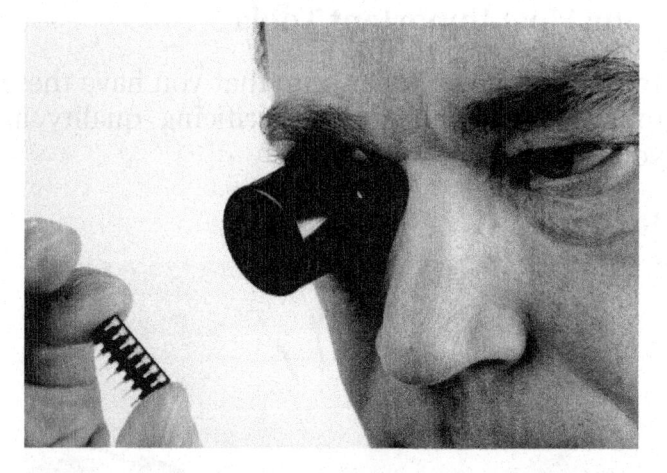

In order to become a reliable watchmaker, you have to clearly see the tiniest parts of the watch.

Eye loupes come in different shapes and sizes, but for starters, you will need these 2 types: General eyeglass with around 3 to 4 times magnification, and inspection eyeglass that can magnify your view up to 12 times. The general eyeglass is mainly used in disassembly and in putting back the pieces of the watch. You will use the inspection eyeglass to take a closer look at the smaller parts, such as the pivots or jewels, or if you need to make sure that you have fixed everything before you fully close the lid.

It's easy to distinguish between eye loupes or eyeglasses because they are numbered. The number equates to the focal length of the glass. For example, No.1 has the capacity to focus an inch from the object. Even if you have clear vision, you need to wear eyeglasses during the process because focusing your eyes on small objects at a near distance can cause eye strain.

To get rid of the problem of constantly holding the eyeglass in place, you can also buy a good wire eyeglass holder. This will make things easier and prevent the eyeglass from accidentally falling onto what you are working on.

3. Screwdriver set

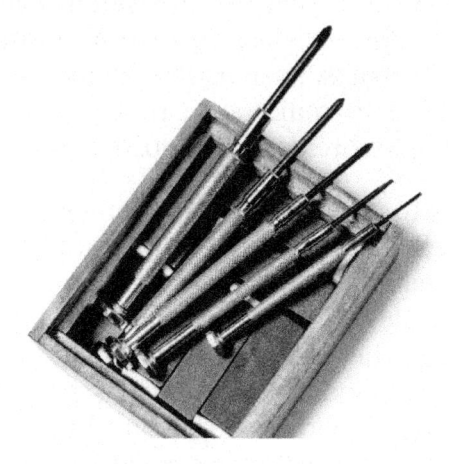

After removing the back of the watch, you will need to disengage the stem in order to completely remove the piece. You also have to remove the remaining screws in the case. Different watches have varying sizes of screws, so you must be equipped with a screwdriver set that has all the sizes you need to get the task done.

There are basically four sizes of screws used for watches, so your repair kit must have the following sizes of screwdrivers: Gray-140, Red-120, Black-100, and Yellow-80. The top manufacturers provide spare blades for each size of screwdriver you buy. They can be trusted when it comes to smoothness and ease of operation, given their ball bearing swivel heads.

Again, buy the best kind because you will use them often. Be wary of cheap offers. Most of them are made of cheap metals that will cause more harm than good on the screws. As much as possible, aim for the known brands that come from Switzerland, which include Horotec, AF Switzerland, and Bergeon.

You can sharpen your screwdrivers with the use of a small jig and a dressing stone. Make sure that you always keep them in good condition. Use an eye loupe when you grind the tools. Each set of screwdriver usually has four to five pieces. You will need another type, the jewel screwdriver, which is used in removing the extra small screws that secure the cap jewels.

4. Tweezers

You need different kinds of tweezers to get the job done. The screwdriver will remove the screw from the watch. The tweezers will pick up the screw, and move the parts of the watch. You cannot use cosmetic tweezers for this purpose.

Your tool must have precise ends. The most important tweezers are those with the following numbers: 2 (comes with hard flat and fine tips), 3 (fine tips), and 5 (tips are short and extra fine, and can be used for hairsprings). Plastic tweezers are only needed if you'll be working on quartz movements and Brass AM as these are prone to scratches.

It is best to buy tweezers that are non-magnetic. It can slow you down when the screws keep on sticking to your tool. Hold the tweezers in between your first two fingers and your thumb, similar to how you hold a pen. Keep on practicing how to hold and use the tool. In time, you will be able to rotate the tweezers 360 degrees without dropping whatever it is that you're holding. Similar to screwdrivers, you have to maintain your tweezers occasionally by grinding the surfaces.

Other Tools You Might Need

After you have invested in the three tools mentioned above, you can then add the following to your watch repair kit:

1. Watch case opener

This tool, which is essentially a specially-crafted knife, can be used for watches with snap-on front and back parts. It comes with a short and rounded blade that you will insert into the chamber of the case, then twist to pop off the cover.

2. Movement holder

After you have removed the movement, you must avoid touching it with your fingers. This is where the movement holder will come in handy. It comes in many sizes and shapes, but the standard type has a reversible feature so you can use it in holding different sizes of movements.

3. Hand lifting levers

One of the most intricate tasks when it comes to watch maintenance and repair is removing the hands. Note that before you can remove the dial, you must first take off the hands. This can be done with either a hand lifting lever or an automatic hand lifting tool. The levers are preferred by many watchmakers because they are able to remove the hands in a vertical manner without causing any damage. The main problem with the hand lifting tool is that it has small plastic feet that push against the dial.

4. Peg wood

This is made from hard wood and is mainly used for holding down the springs and other parts of the watch as you disassemble and reassemble them. It is also used for cleaning the disassembled parts and jewel holes. You can dress the end of the peg wood using a sharp knife to form two of its most typical shapes – flat and pointed. Those who don't have this tool use other alternatives, such as wooden kebab sticks or toothpicks. Always remember that these substitutes are softer than a peg wood and might not hold their form as you go on with the task.

5. Container for watch parts

This will make it easier for you to separate the parts as you disengage and assemble them after. It should help you in keeping the parts, since they are small and are easy to lose. The containers come with covers to keep the parts protected from debris and dust. You don't need to spend a lot for the containers. You can buy the cheap kinds, but look for those that are clear.

6. Degreasing fluid and a glass benzene jar

The best way to clean all the parts of a watch is through the use of a watch cleaning machine. It typically has an ultrasonic feature that can effectively remove dirt, dried oil, and grime from even the smallest parts of the watch. While this is a great tool, this is also expensive. So, as a beginner, you can settle for the next best thing.

You can manually clean parts of the watch using cleaning fluid and a benzene jar. You can still use them even if you have already bought the machine. They can remove the grease quickly when the parts of the watch get contaminated or something in the oiling job went wrong. Choose a benzene jar that has a tight-fitting lid. This will prevent the fluid from evaporating. You can also add a small paintbrush to the set. This will make it easier for you to apply the fluid to the parts of the watch.

7. Greases, oils, oil pots, and oilers

In reassembling the watch parts, it is important to grease the ones where there is friction. The oils will be mostly used in dealing with the escape wheel pivots and balance staff pivots, which are fast moving with low torque. Such lubricants may also have to be applied to the center wheel and barrel arbor, which move slowly with high torque. The grease will be used in dealing with the winding mechanism, canon pinion, hand setting, and other high-speed escapements.

Keep the greases and oils in pots and label them properly. Make sure that all of them have lids to prevent contamination. This way, you are assured that you can use them for a long time.

To get the oils and greases from the pots onto the watch, you will need a watch repair oiler. This is comprised of a metal stem with a colored handle and an end with the shape of a spade. You can get it in four different sizes and it is typically color-coded, such as black for a very fine tip, blue for fine tip, green for medium tip, and red for large tip.

To use the oiler, dip it into the oil and then touch it to the part of the watch that you are repairing. Hold the tool in a vertical manner to allow the oil to slide down even into the smallest crevices. Be sure not to use too much oil, so to be safe, use an oiler with the finest tip. This will make it easier to control the flow. The oiler has to be cleaned when using it in between different kinds of oils. This can be done with the use of a pith wood.

8. Rubber dust blower

It is not recommended to blow the watch parts with your mouth. This could transfer moisture and other elements that may contaminate the parts that you are working on. The rubber dust blower is an affordable tool that can keep dust and dirt away from the smallest parts of the watch, without the risk of getting them contaminated. This can also be used in drying the parts after you have cleaned them.

To use a dust blower, first get a part of the watch from your benzene jar and put it on a piece of paper. Use the tweezers to hold the part in place and blow it dry. Make sure that before using the blower, the grip of the tweezers on the part of the watch is solid and firm. Otherwise, you will risk losing them and since they are small, finding them will be next to impossible.

9. <u>Cleaning putty</u>

This can be used for many purposes, which include removing grime, dirt, fingerprints, and oil from the watch movement. Use this tool like how you would an eraser. Dab the putty on the watch movement to remove the dirt. This can also be used in lifting out hard-to-remove screws and jewels from the movement. This is a useful but inexpensive tool, so it's recommended even for complete beginners.

10. <u>Other tools</u>

Here are the other tools that may come in handy in the craft: a set of needle files, cutting pliers and flat nosed pliers, a small hammer with a steel head that is used for riveting, and another small hammer with a brass head that's used along with the staking tool.

It is also recommended to stock up on balance jewels, timing washers, mainsprings, balance staff, crystal cement, pith, watch papers, plate jewels, jewel cement, and roller jewels. It is better to have these tools ready instead of going out to look them only when you realize you need them. You must always work quickly and efficiently. This way, you can give yourself enough time to inspect your final work before giving it back to your client.

Your Workstation

If you are in the process of planning your workshop, make sure that the windows face north. If this is not possible, you can hang large double-tube fluorescent lamps over the bench, with a distance of around eight feet from the ground. Fit a double-tube fluorescent lamp to your workbench and choose the kind with a long, adjustable arm. This will make it easier for you to move the light in any way you like. Good lighting conditions are necessary in preventing eye strain.

The flooring in your work area must be covered with lightly-colored linoleum. This will make it easier for you to look for any watch parts you have accidentally dropped. Watch repair benches are typically fitted with aprons, and modern benches come with extra-wide aprons, which will help catch any watch parts you might drop. Go for a bench that comes with a wooden top and is painted with white enamel or any light color. Make sure that the top of the bench is always clean. Wash the plate each day before you begin working.

The modern kinds of benches also have drawer spaces where you can place your tools and keep them secured while you are working. This way, the only tools that will remain on top of the bench are the smaller ones, such as the eye loupes, screw drivers, oilers, oil cups, and bench blocks.

You have to arrange your watch repair tools in a way that ensures ease of access. Many horologists prefer to belt the lathe to the motor, but there are some who choose to add a countershaft. You can place a stacking box at the right corner of the bench near the bottom. Arrange the tools that you don't frequently use in the drawers, but keep everything else nearby. You wouldn't want to spend a lot of time searching for a specific tool every time you need it.

Make sure that you also have a comfortable and sturdy chair at your workstation. Choose the kind with an adjustable back and cushion.

Keep your work area well-ventilated. If you have or are planning to put up a watch store, keep it apart from your workstation. It will be easier to work on your own, without the noise and prying eyes that you might encounter when working at the store.

Grinding and Polishing Powders

You will need the following in grinding and polishing the balance pivots, train wheel pivots, and steel parts:

- <u>Oilstone powder</u> – This is a very fine powder that leaves a gray finish. It is applied to the train wheels of watches and small clocks, in order to reduce the square shoulder pivots.
- <u>Carborundum powder</u> – This is available in several grades, but you will only need the finer ones in watchmaking. This is able to cut fast and leaves a coarse and gray finish.
- <u>Diamantine or sapphirine</u> – These can be used for final polishing.

To prepare the abovementioned powders, arrange a three-section polishing block. Put the oilstone powder in the lowest section. Put a small amount on the metal disk, and then add a bit of oil. Mix the two using the blade of a pocket knife. Continue mixing until the consistency becomes similar to a thick paste. Prepare the other oils in the same manner.

The A to Z of Watch Parts

The first chapter talked about the common features found in watches. The following is a list of different watch parts, which you will often deal with as you learn more about watchmaking and as you practice your skills. Make sure that you are familiar with the parts, how they work, and where to find them.

1. Acrylic Crystal

This is also called window or glass, which is a kind of crystal on the front of the timepiece. It serves as protection for the face and the dial. The material is flexible and produces minimal glare when the watch is exposed to light, but this is also less expensive and less durable than other options.

2. Amplitude

It is vital to measure the amplitude of the timepiece because it affects its ability to keep track of time. It refers to the maximum angle that the balance wheel can reach as it swings back and forth.

3. <u>Arbor</u>

This is similar to the post in the center of a carousel, where the gear turns. In watches, this is the axle where the moving parts of the timepiece rotate. This is also referred to as the balance staff.

4. <u>Auxiliary Dial</u>

This is an additional dial found on the face and has different uses depending on the timepiece's complication.

5. <u>Balance Cock</u>

This is a tiny bridge that ensures that the balance wheel is secured in the movement.

6. <u>Balance Spring</u>

It's so fine, which is the reason why it is commonly called hairspring. It coils and recoils. The movement affects the swinging of the balance wheel, which regulates the accuracy of time.

7. <u>Balance Wheel</u>

It moves like how a pendulum works in a clock, in order to divide and regulate time. This is an important part of mechanical watches.

8. Band

It is a metal bracelet that keeps the watch in place while it is worn.

9. Barrel

This is a thin drum for housing the mainspring in mechanical watches. Its size affects the longevity of a watch's power reserve. A double barrel has a longer power reserve than the typical kind.

10. Bezel

This is the ring that surrounds the timepiece's dial. It has various functions that include keeping track of time and measuring both distance and speed. There are watches with bi-directional rotating bezels, which can be rotated clockwise and counterclockwise.

11. Bracelet

It has the same function as the band, but this is composed of links that can be adjusted to the size of the wrist.

12. Breguet Spring

Developed by Breguet in 1795, this was an improvement to the spiral hairspring. The last coil of the spring was raised to make the curve smaller, which minimized wear in balance pivots and improved their rate.

13. Bridge

This refers to the metal plate attached to the main plate, which serves as the frame and holds the gears.

14. Caliber

It has numbers and letters that identify the movement of the watch, as well as and its details.

15. Case

It houses the different parts of a watch and can be made of metal, ceramic, or plastic. The value of a watch increases depending on the material that is used for its case. For example, the ones that are made of plastic are cheaper than the kinds crafted from platinum, silver, rhodium, or gold.

16. Crown

It looks like a knob that is found outside the case. This is used to set the time and other functions. This is also used in winding the mainspring.

17. Crystal

This is a clear cover that serves as the window of the timepiece. It can be made from acrylic, glass, sapphire, or minerals. Among these, sapphire is the most durable, but it's also the most expensive.

18. Deployment Buckle

Also called the foldover, this is a clasp that secures the two ends of the timepiece's bracelet. When opened, it leaves sufficient room to make it easy to glide the watch from the wrist.

19. Dial

This is the face of the timepiece. It is where the time is shown through different indicators and markers.

20. End Shake

The term refers to a worn out jewel hole, which causes the shaking of the arbor.

22. Engine Turned

Also referred to as Guilloche, this is the process of engraving intricate patterns onto the metal parts of the watch with the use of antique machinery.

23. Escapement

It makes sure that the oscillation of the balance wheel remains steady. This is done by providing impulses that control the movement of the hands.

24. Gear Train

This is a system of gears that brings power to the escapement from the mainspring.

25. Incabloc

This works as a shock absorber that ensures that the balance staff of the timepiece will receive less impact when dropped.

26. Lever Escapement

This is included in the movement and is divided into two pallets. Its role is to lock and unlock the teeth of the escape wheel.

27. Lugs

They are found in the case of the timepiece, where the strap, band and bracelet are attached.

28. Main Plate

This serves as the base where the other parts of the movement are placed.

29. Mainspring

This provides power to the gear train of the timepiece.

30. Movement

This is the motor or engine of the watch. The most common types of the movements of watches are automatic, quartz, and mechanical.

31. Plate

This is the front and back part of the case that allows you to inspect the internal parts.

32. Rotor

This is used in automatic watches. It's a flat piece of metal that oscillates to wind the mainspring.

33. Stepping Motor

It moves the gear train in a quartz watch, and thus in turn moves the hands on the dial.

34. Strap

It has the same purpose as a band or bracelet, but this is typically made from fabric, leather, or rubber.

35. Tang Buckle

It looks similar to a belt buckle and is found on most watch straps.

Chapter 3 - Practical Watch Repair (Common Issues & How To Address Them)

Before opening a watch to find out what seems to be the problem, you must first learn how to determine whether a wristwatch needs an overhaul, a temporary repair, or cleaning. To maintain the good condition of your watch, including the classic timepieces, it is essential to have them cleaned once a year.

The following are the three steps that you must perform when a watch suddenly stops working:

1. Test the battery

Even new batteries can become a problem, especially if you had yours replaced at unknown watch repair shops. Buy your own battery from a reputable shop.

Check the contacts on the battery. Any dust or dirt that clings to it can cause malfunction. Use your eye loupe to see clearly. Take the battery out and clean it using a soft cloth. Check the connections and the part of the watch where it is embedded. Make sure that you have gotten rid of any possible cause of the problem before putting back the battery.

2. Check if moisture is causing the problem

Most watches encounter problems when they are damp or moist. These problems typically happen in areas where the weather is icy or rainy.

The problem becomes worse when there is already condensation in the clock face. This can only be addressed through major repair. If it hasn't reached that point yet, check the back for any moisture. Dry it using a hairdryer set on low. Remove the works and blot off excess moisture using a clean cloth. Leave the watch as it is overnight to let it continue to dry. Replace all the parts that you have removed the next day. It should be working by now, or else, you have to continue troubleshooting.

3. Find out if the seals or case is causing the problem

You never know, but the watch may have encountered bumps throughout the day. Take a closer look at the construction of the watch. If it has a winder, check if it is bent, broken, or loose. Waterproof watches have seals and tight screws at the back. Find out if the seal is broken or bent. When a minor repair cannot handle the problem, replace the parts before putting back the pieces again.

Frequently Asked Questions

It is important that you familiarize yourself with the most common questions asked by aspiring horologists:

1. Why did the watch stop?

Improper handling (or dropping) is arguably the main reason why parts come loose and watches stop working. If there doesn't seem to be anything wrong with the watch's externals, the battery could be the culprit.

2. The watch is already a year old, is it time to change the battery even though there are still no problems?

Most modern quartz watches have an end-of-life feature. You will know when it's time to change the battery, so you are not required to do so, unless necessary. This is where the saying, "If it ain't broken, do not fix it," applies. Do not open the watch unless it's really necessary to do so because it compromises the factory seals. It may cause more problems that could have been avoided had you not resorted to opening the case.

3. Why does the second hand skip several times during the day?

This is an indication that the battery is about to drain. Likewise, it serves as a warning that the voltage is getting low.

4. What's the problem when the watch doesn't run and the second hand just moves back and forth?

This is an indication that the watch is electronically functional, but its mechanical portion is not working. The problem here is the watch movement, and it's usually repaired through extensive maintenance and cleaning.

5. The alarm of the watch stopped working after the battery was changed. What caused the problem?

This can be caused by many factors, the most common of which is when the contact spring of the alarm loses its proper place. Before opening the watch to see if this is what's causing the problem, ensure that the back of the case is properly installed. The next thing that you ought to check is if there is a problem with the contact plate of the alarm.

6. <u>Using the chronograph seems to drain the battery faster than it should. What needs to be done in this case?</u>

Leaving the chronograph function on even when it is not running will really reduce battery life. Bear in mind that the indicated battery life is only for the basic timekeeping function. It is best to stop the chronograph or stopwatch function when it is not in use, in order to conserve battery.

7. <u>Why does the watch stop working when worn, but runs smoothly when it is not in use?</u>

This indicates that the electronic circuitry of the watch is defective. It reacts to your body temperature, so it stops working when worn. The increase in temperature causes a slight expansion that leads to the problem. Perform a routine maintenance on the watch and replace the circuit.

8. <u>The numbers and letters shown on the digital display are not complete. How do you fix the issue?</u>

The points that connect the circuitry to the digital display may have corroded. As a result, not enough voltage is sent to the display segment, which makes the numbers and letters unrecognizable. Repairing the watch with this problem can be costly. You have to explain it to your clients, so that they can decide if they will continue to have the item repaired. It is not recommended for fashion watches because the cost of the repair may be higher than buying a new watch.

9. <u>The numbers in the digital display cannot be read and it has turned completely black. How do you fix this?</u>

This can be caused by a drop that sent a severe shock to the watch. The digital display has become contaminated or has cracked. The conductive fluid in the glass may have been damaged due to air leakage. This is another costly repair since the glass needs to be replaced, so you have to explain to your clients their options before proceeding with it.

10. <u>What is causing the buttons to get stuck?</u>

There is a stem attached to the underside of the push buttons on a watch. The stem moves in and out of the tube when de-pressed. There is also a little spring that pushes the stem back to its original position once the button is released. With continued use of the watch, dirt can accumulate inside the tube. This will cause the spring to get stuck and it won't be able to move back to its original position even after the button is released.

The right way to handle the problem depends on how critical it is. In some cases, cleaning would be sufficient. However, if the problem has caused the spring to break, you will need to replace it. To ensure that everything is fixed and it will take longer before anything like this happens again, it is best to carry out a complete maintenance routine.

Other Common Problems and How to Fix Them

Before opening a watch of any make, it is your responsibility to assess the situation. You have to make your clients understand the pros and cons of the process. There are certain clients who will insist on having their fancy watches repaired despite the odds.

To help you become more prepared, here are other common problems that you might encounter:

Problems Related to the Mainspring

You have to find out the kind of mainspring that the watch has and what seems to be the problem, so that you can effectively come up with a solution.

1. Swiss mainsprings – The most common problem with these springs is they don't always hook well with the barrel, although shaping and filling the end of the tongue should solve it. If this doesn't work, use a long pointed graver to undercut the step in the barrel. Make sure that

the end of the step is not rounded and it fits the cap properly.

2. Mainspring gauges – There are currently two types of gauges used for the mainspring, namely the metric and the Dennison. Between the two, many horologists prefer the metric because it allows for closer measurements. You can measure the width using a Vernier gauge and use the metric micrometer to measure the thickness.

3. Hook and barrel – There are instances when the hook is broken and doesn't fit the barrel anymore, indicating the need for replacement. Remember the following pointers in making a new hook:

- Keep it as narrow as possible.
- It has to be strong, meaning it's capable of resisting strain once the spring is fully wound.
- It should be able to secure the spring against the barrel wall.

To make a new hook, you must first drill a hole in the barrel. Make sure that the distance of the hole from the cap is fully centered in the inner part of the barrel. Use a small tap in threading the hole. File a piece of light steel wire to a small taper with the use of a pin vise. Create a thread with the screw plate using the same wire (use the bigger part of the taper). Be sure it matches the size of the hole. After you are done with a full thread, cut off the wire but leave enough height to file the hook according to its right shape. Make sure that the wire stays in the screw plate.

After you have filed the hook, get the wire off from the screw plate. Screw it in the barrel coming from the inner part. Tighten it before cutting off the wire. Inspect the hole at the outermost part of the spring. Do not spring it too far. Punch a hole, leaving around 2mm of the spring outside of the hole. Curve this part in a slight manner until it is conformed to the circle of the barrel wall. The hole has to fit freely on the hook.

4. Cap and barrel – Fitting the cap to the barrel isn't always easy. You have to make sure that the barrel cap will stay put. If you are having a problem with it, lightly file the cap's circumference. When the glazed surface gets rough, the cap will have an easier time keeping its position.

5. Stems – Fitting the stem isn't necessary for watches that come with factory stems. You will only need to make the stem shorter in order to get the right height for the crown. To do that, you must first check the size of the pivot by putting a small drill in the bearing. This will turn the pivot to the needed size. Use an escapement file to reduce the square by holding the stem in a pin vase.

6. Broken screws – This can really be problematic, especially when the remaining part of the screw will not move no matter what you do. First, you can try filing the slot using a screw head file before dealing with the remaining part of the screw using a screwdriver. If this doesn't work, make a solution composed of five parts water and one part alum. Make sure that the solution is mixed well before you submerge all the steel parts of the watch in it. Leave it for 12 hours. The problematic screw will dissolve in the solution, leaving the parts that are made of nickel or brass, such as the plates, intact. If the screw is still undissolved, leave it in the solution for the rest of the day or add more hours, if you deem it necessary.

How to Repair the Train

Most of your tasks as a horologist will include closing the holes in bridges and plates. How you deal with them depends on how badly worn the holes are. A staking tool is enough to fix holes with minor issues. Use a stump with a flat surface to put the bridge or plate in the die of your tool's frame.

Now choose a punch with a round end. Fit this in the oil cup and be careful in tapping the hole. Make sure that the pivot will not be pushed too far. Raise the hole and place the wheel in between the plates. Make sure that the end shake has around one third of the pivot's diameter. You can use a friction jeweling machine for watches that are fixed using friction brushings. For watches without friction brushings, you can replace the unnecessary end shake by creating a small hollow in the face to remodel a stump.

Once you have closed the hole, you will notice that the metal in the plate has sunk in the hollow of the stump. This will lessen the end shake. Reverse the procedure if you observe that the end shake looks too tight.

How would you know that you have dealt with the problem? Consider it solved when the wheel is able to spin freely in between the dial-down and dial-up positions. In cases when the escape wheel seems to be worn beyond repair, deal with it by performing friction jeweling.

How to Do Friction Jeweling

This is what you need to do when there is a V-shaped depression in place of a hole piercing jewel. Jewels have long been employed in clocks and watches, such as the bezel-type jewels, which were gradually replaced since the introduction of friction-type jewels in 1920.

1. Replacing bezel-type jewels

Since many are predicting that bezel-type jewels will soon be obsolete, here's how you can replace one with a friction jewel. Measure the depth required for the jewel to be given enough end shake, and use the right machine to accomplish the task. Place the pusher on the jewel that you will replace. Make an adjustment on the metric screw at the top part of the machine. Your goal is for the new jewel to be placed at the same depth as the broken one. Push out the latter and use the smallest reamer to give the plate a straight and clean hole. Choose the right jewel – the outer diameter should be 1/100 of a millimeter bigger than the hole in the plate. You can check the hole's size on the stamping on the reamer last used.

Use the wheel countersinks in removing the burr that was left behind by the reamer. Put the jewel in the hole with the bottom facing up. This will easily glide even without the help of a machine. Push the jewel by lowering the pusher – be sure to use just enough pressure. Once the jewel is in place, the metric stop will arrest the movement when you have reached the right depth.

2. Replacing a friction jewel

If the watch has a friction jewel that needs to be replaced, you must get the measurement of the hole in the plate by using a special gauge or a reamer. Once done, get the jewel and push it according to the right depth.

3. Fitting the jewel in a removable setting.

This is typically done in the cap jewel and the case of a balance. Use special tools that can be connected to the machine to hold the setting while the reaming is in progress.

Learning the craft of watchmaking is also ideal for those who love collecting antique watches. The repair and maintenance for such timepieces are costly. If, on the other hand, you're planning to sell watches by setting up your own store, these skills will also come in handy. You could offer repair and maintenance services to your clients and they no longer need to look for service centers.

More Practical Tips about Watchmaking

There are many reasons that you can further look into when the watch stops or if it stops from time to time. It will be easier to spot the problem after you have gained enough experience. Practical application will allow you to understand the intricacies of the construction of a watch.

If the watch fails to work even after you have tested the battery, check if any of the following is causing the problem:

- The mainspring isn't properly set
- The minute or hour wheel may be tight
- The roller jewel may be loose, or it may be too long
- There may be some rusty parts, such as the escape wheel teeth or pinions
- They may be worn holes or cracked jewels in the bridges and plates
- The center wheel may have gotten into contact with the balance wheel

The problem can also be caused the sweep second hand, which is a common feature in modern wristwatches. You have to be extra careful in dealing with it. The usual culprit is the height of the crystal. It may not be meeting the required height and it is not able to provide the needed clearance. This is also the reason why the watch would run smoothly, unless when worn on the wrist. Once worn, the second hand of the watch vibrates. It touches the minute hand or crystal, which makes the watch stop and start again when you remove it from your wrist.

Here are some more things that you must look into when the watch has an irregular rate:

- The balance motion may be too short or too long
- The cannon pinion is loose
- The balance spring is being pinched by the regulator pins
- Magnetism
- The balance is out of poise
- The regulator pins are spread farther apart than necessary

If you have checked the watch's construction and it's actually good and clean, the most likely reason for the erratic rate is the shortness of its balance motion. This can be caused by setting the spring or mainspring at an incorrect length.

Chapter 4 - Cleaning & Reassembling A Watch

It takes a lot of practice before you can perfect the skills in maintaining and reassembling watches. The information in this book will only serve as your guide. This will give you ideas of what to expect and tell you what to do, but the real learning process begins when you start practicing what you have learned.

Maintenance and Reassembly Techniques

Here are the basic things you need to learn and some pointers on what to do:

<u>Cleaning and oiling</u>

1. Remove the movement from the case

This is the first thing that you need to work on and master – take the pieces of the watch apart, then examine each one closely and determine their purpose. In order to do that, you must first know how to remove the movement from the case. This is not as simple as it sounds. You have to move in a delicate manner and be aware that one wrong move could break the parts.

For snap-on cases with a back and a bezel, you must first release and then click. Allow the crown to gently slip between your thumb and first finger as you let the mainspring down. Position the watch with the train side up on your bench, and then give the screw a couple of turns in order to release the stem. Once done, you can pull out the stem and remove the screws from the case. This will make it easier to push the movement out.

The procedure above applies to majority of cases, but certain older makes of American watches may have a different construction. You will need to pull out the stem to the position of setting the hands. Get the case screws out and push the movement, leaving the stem, sleeve, and crown in the case – unless these parts need to be replaced.

The cases of most modern wristwatches come with a two-piece construction. Use the case opener in prying off the bezel and then lift the movement out by twisting the blade using a screwdriver.

Opening water-resistant cases requires different kinds of tools. For example, to open a timepiece with three-piece construction, you have to remove the case first before you can take the movement out. There are also water-resistant cases where you will need to pry off an unbreakable crystal to open the case. Use cutting pliers to pull out the stem. There are also cases where you need to press the crystal down to release the back part.

The idea here is to study the construction of the case before you proceed in removing the movement. Take a lot of caution, especially in dealing with cases that look unfamiliar.

2. Disassembling the movement

Place the movement in the holder with the train side up. Change the stem and tighten the screw. Take the balance out from the lower plate as you remove the balance spring on the bridge. Secure the balance on a hole of your bench block. This way, you can avoid possible accidents that may happen to the pivots after you have cleaned the balance.

Proceed in removing the other parts of the watch in this order:

- Use a hand remover to disengage the hands.

- Take the dial out, followed by the hour and minute hands.

- Use a cannon pinion remover to pull out the cannon pinion.

- Take the lever and the pallet bridge out after the mainspring has been let down.

- Remove the crown wheels, ratchet, train bridges, barrel bridge, train wheels, and the mainspring barrel.

- Place the barrel on your bench block with the cap facing up.

- Pry it off using a small screwdriver.

  Note: The most common accident that happens in this phase is the mainspring and arbor flying out, so you must always perform this with gentleness and caution.

- Use heavy tweezers to carefully remove the arbor. Once it is turned, you can unhook the mainspring to remove the arbor, and then remove the mainspring after.

- Before you remove the cap jewels, make sure that you mark the settings of the jewel and the plate to make it easier for you to place the parts back in their original positions.

3. Cleaning the watch

Tie the bridges and lower plate using a looped wire and immerse them in a jar filled with watch-cleaning solution. Leave it for a couple of minutes. Dip a brush in the cleaning solution and use this in brushing the parts. Rinse them in warm water. You will then dry them by dipping them in alcohol, or you could also use a drying solution that specifically made for this purpose. Put the parts in warm boxwood sawdust and shake until dry.

Tie the wheels in a looped wire and follow the rest of the steps above. If the mainspring is not set, you can use this again, else you will need to fit a new spring. Clean the mainspring by following the same steps outlined above.

What about the smaller parts of the watch that will be difficult to tie? Fill a shallow container with watch-cleaning solution. This is where you will put the small parts, such as the screws, lever, and jewels. Remove the parts one at a time using special tweezers intended for small items. Once they are soaked in the cleaning solution, get them one at a time and hold them against a hard pith. Use a soft brush to clean them. Dip them in a drying solution afterwards and transfer to a piece of paper to completely dry. You can clean the jewels further by twisting the pointed tip of a pegwood in the hole. Use a pegwood with a flat end in cleaning the cap jewels.

Clean the balance separately. Place the pivots in a piece of hard pith and examine them closely using an appropriate eye loupe. You can clean the pivots by dipping them in a special cleaning solution until they look polished and smooth. Dip them next in a drying solution, and put them in sawdust and shake to dry. For balance pivots that look tarnished, you can dip them first in cyanide of potassium before cleaning them thoroughly. The last part must be done with extreme caution since cyanide is a poison. You can polish the pivots in the lathe if they are badly corroded.

4. Putting back the movement in place

Place the cap jewels back. Insert a tiny wire in the hole jewel before pouring a bit of watch oil in each hole. Using an eye loupe, examine the size of the oil bubble that forms. Put more oil until the required bubble size is met. If the hole jewel is flat, you will not get the right size of bubble. The hole has to be corrected in this instance. If whole cap jewel gets covered by the bubble, you need to remove it, clean it, and put it back again.

You have to get the right amount of oil in the holes to ensure that the watch will function well until the next period of cleaning. Put the balance in a flat and level manner on the lower plate.

Put oil on all surfaces of the winding mechanism that are subjected to friction. Put the mainspring in the barrel through the use of a mainspring winder before putting sufficient watch oil. Focus on the escape wheel. Push its pinion end against a piece of hard pith before oiling every other tooth of the wheel. Put the train wheels and barrel on the lower plate. Make sure that the bridges fit before screwing them down. Test the wheels – none should show excessive shaking, but the center, third, and fourth wheels should shake a bit more than the escape wheel.

Put oil on the train jewels. Test the lever after winding the mainspring. Put the balance and watch closely if it will show a good motion. If it does, then you are done with the task.

<u>Using a Watch-Cleaning Machine</u>

More advanced shops and hobbyists utilize watch-cleaning machines instead of using sawdust in the cleaning process. The machine has four jars, where you will put the drying and cleaning solutions, and a basket, where you will place the parts of the watch. The basket is attached to an electric motor.

To use the machine, first disassemble the parts of the watch and put them in the basket. Arrange them in a way that the smaller parts are on the top, and the bigger ones are at the bottom. Put the pivots in a hard pith and clean them. Put the balance in the small spaces at the top part of the basket. Place a crumpled piece of tissue paper on top of the balance to avoid any mishap.

You will then lower the basket into the jar that has the cleaning solution. Run the motor at a moderate speed for several minutes. Raise the basket and shake it a bit to get rid of all the used solution. Now, it's time to lower the basket into the jar that contains the rinsing solution. Be sure to remove all traces of the solution by raising the basket and shaking it once more. Repeat the process on the second rinsing solution. After this, let the basket spin in the container with a small heater and allow the watch parts to dry.

How to Polish the Pivots

You can address common pivot issues by following these steps:

1. Train wheel pivots

You will need to place a new wheel on the timepiece when the pivots are badly cut. It happens as a result of dirty pivot holes or cracked and damaged jewels. Determine if a new wheel is necessary or if the pivot needs some polishing and may have to be reduced, such as in the case of pivot in the center wheel.

To repair the short pivot in the center wheel, put the pinion in a split chuck. Adjust accordingly until the pivot is corrected. Turn it down using a graver until it is laid straight. Ensure that the shoulder where it meets doesn't have a round edge. This will not happen if the graver that you are using is well-sharpened.

Cross-file the two sides of the iron slip. Grind the pivot with the use of oil and oilstone powder until you have a gray finish. Use a steel burnisher to finish the material further. Polish the ball metal slip using oil and diamantine.

2. Balance pivots

How you deal with a damaged balance pivot will depend on its condition. If it is burred, use a jasper stone to reduce its cylindrical part. Touch its end and slightly round its corner. Use a steel burnisher to burnish the pivot and roll it after from the cylindrical area to the end. This way, the corner will have less chances of getting burred. Polish the cylindrical portion using a diamantine or a boxwood slip.

In cases when the pivot needs to be reduced, you must also fit a new staff into the scheme. After reducing the pivot until the jewel already fits, reduce this to a free fit using a jasper slip.

How to Deal with Balance Assembly Repairs

1. Remove the balance spring

Put the balance on your bench block and hold it tightly using your first two fingers. Put a screwdriver under the point opposite the spring's pinning point. Twist the screwdriver to remove the spring.

2. Remove the roller table

This is done with the help of a roller remover. Use a hollow punch fitted to the lower part of the pivot. Use a brass hammer to tap them lightly, which is enough to remove the roller.

3. Remove the worn staff

This will depend on the kind of staff that you want to remove. The balance staff comes in two types – friction and riveted. For the latter, make sure that you don't create any damage to the hole in the wheel. Turn off the riveted portion before removing the hub.

In dealing with the removal of the friction type, make sure that the hub lays on the die of your staking tool. If you will go on with the process without seeing to it that the position is right, the hub is likely to get pushed out along with the staff.

4. Fitting a new staff

You must have the right model of staff before you try to fit it in. For the riveted type, choose the hole in the die of your staking tool where the roller axis will fit freely. Choose the hollow punch with a round face and fit this on the collet axis before you rivet the staff to its wheel. This can be done with up to three light taps using a brass hammer. Move the wheel to even out the riveting process and use a flat-faced hollow punch to finish it. You can easily fit a friction type of staff by following how the old one was installed.

5. Adapting the balance to the timepiece

The balance jewels should have minimal side shake when fitted freely. Still, the pivots must protrude sufficient through the jewels. Put the new cap jewels before trying out if the balance is already working fine. If it isn't, you can adjust the end shake by bending the balance bridge or making the pivots shorter. Whatever you do, make sure that the balance bridge is constantly in line with the lower plate.

<u>How to Set the Roller Jewel</u>

A roller jewel of a timepiece can get lost or broken. If it is lost, carefully inspect the part using your pivot eye loupe. Put the lever on a piece of hard pith. You will then try to replace the missing jewel in the fork slot. Make sure that the replacement is of the right size and has the proper freedom once set.

Once you have the right replacement for the missing roller jewel, put the roller table in between the jaws of your combination tool. Heat the end of the tool by flaming it with an alcohol lamp. Once the roller table is hot enough, place a small amount of shellac on its back, directly over the jewel hole. Put the roller jewel while the shellac is still soft. When that's done, heat the roller table once more. Before the shellac hardens, straighten the jewel using your tweezers until it is in line with the staff and in an upright position.

How to Poise the Balance

The only tool that you can use to get this done is the three-legged poising tool with two adjustable legs. Start by putting the balance on the attached roller table. Reduce the weight of the balance by using special cutters on the heavy side of the material. You can also add balance washers to the lighter part of the material.

A hollow tube is typically found around the tool used for reducing weight. The tubes come in different sizes. You will use the one that has the same size as the balance screw. Secure the balance using the balance clamp to begin using the weight-reducing tools. Press down the cutter on top of the balance screws. Turn the screw using a screwdriver until it is hollowed out and forms a V-shape.

Using a poising saw on the slot in the screw deeper is also an option if you need to reduce the weight. Arrange the blade in a lengthwise manner on a medium file. Tap the blade sharply using a small hammer until teeth that can cut the balance screw are formed. To add weight, you need to lightly loosen the screw using a screwdriver and remove it using a balance screw holder.

Put the washer at the end of the balance to have the screw replaced. The task is done when the balance is already in a satisfactory poise, which means that it can be halted at any point.

How to True the Balance Springs

This is for the more advanced horologists. It takes years of practice to perfect this part of the process, so make sure that you spend a lot of time doing this while you are still beginning to learn about the craft.

Take all the opportunities to practice how to balance the spring work, even if it means that you will work on the old and broken pieces of watches. Also, this is where a good pair of tweezers will really come in handy. The tweezers must have fine points, but you must also use tweezers with straight points and another with curved points.

To begin truing in the round, put the balance into the attached balance spring in the brass calipers. Fit the friction jewels in the ends for the calipers to become more effective. Turn the balance by following the coils that surround the collet.

After this, learn the process of truing in the flat and making the spring adapt to the watch. Take your time in learning everything that you need to know about the process.

Chapter 5 – Proper Winding & Maintenance

There are two basic methods of winding a watch. The method that you need to perform will depend on the kind of watch you are dealing with.

1. <u>How to wind a watch with manual movement</u>

Refrain from winding a watch while it is still on the wrist. The motion may not be effective since the item is still snug to the skin. To begin the task, lay the watch on a flat surface. Locate the stem and pull it out. The stem may be intended for different complications, so push and pull until you have set it for winding.

Be careful in pulling out the stem. Too much force can cause the over-winding of the mechanism. Wind in a clockwise manner until you feel the resistance. How would you know that you have done sufficient winding? The watch should be able to run smoothly for the intended period. There are certain makes that last for a week with one wind. This kind of information–how long should the watch run after each wind–can be seen in its packaging details. You can also get the serial code and search online. If it slows down sooner than usual, this means that you were not able to hit the maximum tension.

The number of turns that needs to be done when winding a manual watch depends on its size. Ideally, it should be about 20 to 40 turns. Once you are done, push the crown back to its original position. The watch should start running again when all the components are in place.

2. How to set a watch with an automatic movement

A watch with an automatic movement will run for a long time without winding. Winding it would only be necessary if it hasn't been worn for a long time. Since it might stop from non-use, so you have to manually wind the watch to set the time.

To begin winding this kind of watch, look for the stem at its side. Be careful in handling the stem because it is connected to other important mechanisms inside, which could be damaged due to improper handling of the stem. It is also not advisable to fiddle with the stem while the watch is still on the wrist because you might accidentally bend and break it.

Look for the crown. This is powered by a rotor, but aside from that, it looks a lot like a manual movement watch. Pull out the crown until the stem is exposed. Begin winding the crown by twisting it in a clockwise manner until there's resistance. Stop at this point and put the crown back in its original position. After winding the watch, you can already set its other functions, such as the time and date.

<u>Important Reminders about Winding</u>

If the watch needs to be wound every day, make sure that you don't forget to perform the task. Make it a routine – something that you will do before you sleep or soon after you have woken up. A fully-wound watch will give accurate time for approximately 18 to 36 hours. The duration will depend on the size of the timepiece's mechanism.

You have to wind a mechanical watch at least once a week, even when it is not in use. This way, you can be sure it will run smoothly when you finally need to wear it.

Top Tips in Caring for a Watch

As a horologist, it will come in handy if you will give tips to your clients on how to properly care for their watches. Here are the top tips that you can give your clients:

1. Watches must be stored properly when not in use. Use a protective coating, like a bubble wrap or a soft fabric, to wrap the timepiece before putting it in its dedicated storage. Put it somewhere cool and clean. You wouldn't want it to acquire moisture and dust while it is not in use. Never forget to wind the watch according to the directions, even when it is in storage.

2. Always move the hands in a clockwise manner when you are setting the time and other functions of the watch.

3. To ensure the longevity of a mechanical watch, it has to be serviced every three years. If you observe that the watch is showing signs of malfunction, have it serviced even if you still haven't hit the three-year mark. A quartz watch, on the other hand, should be serviced every four years.

4. Avoid placing your timepiece anywhere near magnets because they can affect the timekeeping mechanism of the material.

5. You have to be aware of your timepiece's water resistance. Do not test if it can handle more than what it is capable of. A quick change

in pressure may be too much to handle for the material. Even watches that are not water resistant can handle occasional splashes of water, but make sure that it doesn't happen often. Here's a brief guide about the water-resistance capacity of watches:

- 30 meters – This is more often tagged simply as water resistant and can only handle occasional splashing.
- 50 meters – You can wear it while swimming, but do not immerse the watch for a long time.
- 100 meters – You can use this in all kinds of swimming activities for as long as you like.
- 200 meters – The watch can be safely used while diving.
- 200 meters and above – The timepiece can be used for deep diving.

6. Take good care of the crystal. Keep it safe from impact in order to avoid scratches and other damages.

7. Have a proper storage for your watches. If you don't want to buy special storage boxes, you can keep the timepiece in its original box. Your goal here is to keep the crystal protected from scratches and for the watch to avoid getting dirty while it is not in use.

8. Make sure that you avoid the timepiece from getting in contact with chemicals. There are strong chemicals that can damage the metals and the band, such as cleaning agents and perfume or cologne. If you have sprayed perfume or cologne on your wrist, allow it to completely dry before putting on your watch.

9. Avoid too much exposure to the sun. Heat can shorten a watch's battery (unless it is solar powered). Likewise, the heat of the sun can make the color of the timepiece fade easily. It is best to avoid exposing the material to direct sunlight.

Conclusion

I hope this book was able to help you become more driven to learn about watchmaking. Make sure that you practice what you have learned. Buy the needed gear and equipment, and begin by cleaning and performing little repairs on your watches. You will get the hang of it in time. Grab all the opportunities to learn more about the process. You never know, but the hobby can become a profitable venture in the future.

Thank you for purchasing this book!

CPSIA information can be obtained
at www.ICGtesting.com
Printed in the USA
BVOW06s0212241117
501171BV00017B/127/P

9 781541 230682